STORY 1: A LONELY FLORIST RESOLVES TO FIND LOVE BY 11:59 P.M. ON VALENTINE'S DAY.

STORY 2: A FIREFIGHTER'S HEART BURNS WHENEVER HE DRIVES HIS TRUCK PAST ONE PARTICULAR HOUSE IN THE LOCAL AREA.

STORY 3: TWO TEENAGERS FROM WARRING TRIBES MUST PLAN HOW TO FLEE TOGETHER WITHOUT COMING TO HARM.

STORY 4: A PROPERTY DEVELOPER FALLS IN LOVE WITH AN ENVIRONMENTALIST WHILST RESEARCHING A POTENTIAL DEVELOPMENT SITE.

STORY 5: AN AUTHOR DELIVERS A BOOK TO THE TOWN LIBRARY, BUT SHE ONLY WANTS ONE OF THE LIBRARIANS TO READ IT.

STORY 6: A COUPLE OF PET SITTERS ACCIDENTALLY GET THEIR DOG LEADS TANGLED ON A MORNING WALK.

STORY 7: A SPINSTER MARRIES A DIFFERENT MAN IN HER DREAMS EVERY NIGHT.

_____

_____

_____

_____

_____

_____

_____

_____

_____

_____

_____

_____

_____

_____

_____

_____

_____

Story 8: A game developer cannot seem to complete his project of designing his ideal girlfriend.

Story 9: A small town guy and city girl agree to swap places for a week.

_____

_____

_____

_____

_____

_____

_____

_____

_____

_____

_____

_____

_____

_____

_____

_____

_____

_____

_____

Story 10: An illiterate rural farmer receives love notes that he cannot yet understand.

Story 11: A dentist realizes that she has managed to engineer the perfect smile for one of her patients.

_____

_____

_____

_____

_____

_____

_____

_____

_____

_____

_____

_____

_____

_____

_____

_____

_____

_____

_____

_____

_____

_____

STORY 12: A WATCH FIXER WILL ONLY AGREE TO REPAIR THE WATCH OF ONE CUSTOMER.

_____

_____

_____

_____

_____

_____

_____

_____

_____

_____

_____

_____

_____

_____

_____

_____

_____

_____

_____

_____

_____

Story 13: A health blogger is searching for someone who can supply her with an exercise routine to make her invincible.

_____

_____

_____

_____

_____

_____

_____

_____

_____

_____

_____

_____

_____

_____

_____

_____

_____

_____

_____

_____

_____

_____

Story 14: The same love story unfolds simultaneously in two different continents.

STORY 15: AN ADVENTURER DISCOVERS A CAVE WITH MAGIC IN THE AIR, WHICH CAN BE BOTTLED AND SOLD TO HEARTBROKEN PEOPLE.

Story 16: A café owner names her new coffee brand 'Stephen's Favorite.' People ask her who Stephen is, but she refuses to say.

_____

_____

_____

_____

_____

_____

_____

_____

_____

_____

_____

_____

_____

_____

_____

_____

_____

_____

_____

_____

_____

_____

Story 17: A ninja must figure out what to buy his wife for their anniversary that shows he still cares for her.

_____

_____

_____

_____

_____

_____

_____

_____

_____

_____

_____

_____

_____

_____

_____

_____

_____

_____

_____

_____

_____

_____

STORY 18: A COUPLE ARE ONLY ALLOWED TO KISS DURING THUNDERSTORMS. THEY TRAVEL AROUND THE WORLD CHASING BAD WEATHER.

STORY 19: A BANKER KEEPS A PRIVATE SAVINGS ACCOUNT THAT SHE VOWS NOT TO WITHDRAW CASH FROM UNTIL HER EX-PARTNER TALKS TO HER.

STORY 20: A GARDENER IS STARRY EYED WHEN A SHOP ASSISTANT HELPS HIM UP AFTER A BAG OF SOIL FALLS ON HIM AT THE GARDEN CENTER.

STORY 21: A HIKER CLIMBS THE SAME MOUNTAIN ON THE 1ST OF JUNE EVERY YEAR WITH A PICNIC BASKET. HE HOPES TO MEET SOMEONE THERE.

STORY 22: A SKETCHER DRAWS THREE SIMILAR LOOKING MEN IN EXQUISITE DETAIL, EXCEPT THEY EACH HAVE SOMETHING MISSING – THEIR HEARTS.

STORY 23: A CINEMA OWNER REFUSES TO STOP SHOWING "THE NOTEBOOK" ON SCREEN 4 AT LEAST ONCE A WEEK.

STORY 24: TWO SPACE TRAVELERS MUST FIND SOMEBODY THAT CAN OFFICIALLY MARRY THEM.

STORY 25: A CLEANER STEALS PHOTO FRAMES OF THE COUPLE WHOSE HOUSE SHE CLEANS. SHE SELLS THEM AT A CAR BOOT SALE.

STORY 26: A HISTORIAN RESOLVES TO REWRITE THE WORLD'S HISTORY SO THAT HER BOYFRIEND DOES NOT THINK THE WORLD IS SUCH A BAD PLACE.

STORY 27: AN ARCHITECT CONSTRUCTS A BESPOKE CASTLE, BECAUSE THE PRINCESS HE IS IN LOVE WITH REFUSES TO DOWNSIZE.

STORY 28: A MASSEUSE DOES NOT FIND HER MOST REGULAR CLIENT EASY ON THE EYES, BUT SHE LOVES THE FEEL OF HIS SKIN.

STORY 29: A GRAVE DIGGER BUYS AN EXPENSIVE SUIT FOR TONIGHT'S WORK.

_____

_____

_____

_____

_____

_____

_____

_____

_____

_____

_____

_____

_____

_____

_____

_____

_____

_____

_____

STORY 30: A WEDDING PLANNER DECIDES THAT THEY WILL ONLY GET MARRIED ON ONE CONDITION.

_____

_____

_____

_____

_____

_____

_____

_____

_____

_____

_____

_____

_____

_____

_____

_____

_____

_____

_____

_____

_____

_____

STORY 31: A SPECIALIST CHEF WOWS CUSTOMERS WITH HIS FOOD, BUT THE WOMAN HE WANTS TO IMPRESS THE MOST STORMS OUT THE RESTAURANT.

STORY 32: A BEAUTICIAN FINDS LOVE TOO UGLY TO BEAR AFTER A FREAK ACCIDENT AT THE SALON.

_____

_____

_____

_____

_____

_____

_____

_____

_____

_____

_____

_____

_____

_____

_____

_____

_____

_____

_____

_____

_____

_____

STORY 33: A PSYCHIC KNOWS THEY WILL DIE SOON, AND MUST DECIDE WHETHER IT IS MORALLY ACCEPTABLE TO FIND LOVE BEFORE THEY PASS.

www.ingramcontent.com/pod-product-compliance
Lightning Source LLC
Chambersburg PA
CBHW020326290526
45785CB00007B/2934